DATE DUE

8-6-19			

DEMCO 38-296

Neale Donald Walsch

on

RELATIONSHIPS

Books by Neale Donald Walsch

Conversations with God, Book 1

Conversations with God, Book 2

Conversations with God, Book 3

Conversations with God, Book 1 Guidebook

Meditations from Conversations with God, Book 1

Meditations from Conversations with God, Book2:
A Personal Journal

The Little Soul and the Sun

Questions and Answers on Conversations with God

Neale Donald Walsch on Abundance and Right
Livelihood

Neale Donald Walsch on Holistic Living

Friendship with God

Applications for Living

Neale Donald Walsch
on
RELATIONSHIPS

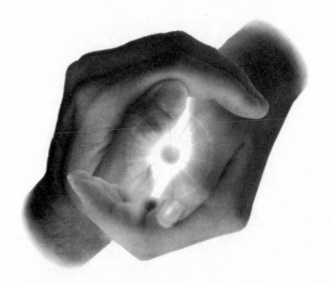

Neale Donald Walsch

HAMPTON ROADS
PUBLISHING COMPANY, INC.
for the evolving human spirit

Cover design by Marjoram Productions
Cover art by Matthew and Jonathan Friedman

For information write:

Hampton Roads Publishing Company, Inc.
134 Burgess Lane
Charlottesville, VA 22902

Or call: 804-296-2772
FAX: 804-296-5096
e-mail: hrpc@hrpub.com
Web site: http://www.hrpub.com

If you are unable to order this book from your local
bookseller, you may order directly from the publisher.
Quantity discounts for organizations are available.
Call 1-800-766-8009, toll-free.

Library of Congress Catalog Card Number: 99-95399

ISBN 1-57174-163-1

10 9 8 7 6 5 4 3 2 1

Printed on acid-free paper in the United States

Dedication

Again, to Nancy.

Every definition of
Wonderful Relationship
is embodied in her.

If you knew her, you would
not have to read another book,
play another tape, hear another sermon,
ask another question.
All you would have to do
is watch her.

Introduction

Relationship is the most important experience of our lives. Without it, we are nothing.

Literally.

That is because, in the absence of anything else, *we* are not.

Fortunately, there is not a one of us who does not have a relationship. Indeed, all of us are in relationship with everything and everyone, all of the time. We have a relationship with ourselves, we have a relationship with our family, we have a relationship with our environment, we have a relationship with our work, we have a relationship with each other.

In fact, everything that we know and experience about ourselves, we understand within the context that is created by our relationships. For this reason, relationships are sacred. All relationships. And somewhere within the deepest reaches of our heart and soul, we know this. That is why we yearn so for relationships—and for relationships of meaning. It is also, no doubt, why we have such trouble with them. At some level, we must be very clear how much is at stake. And so, we're nervous about them. Normally confident, competent people fumble and fall, stumble and stall, crumble and call for help.

Indeed, nothing has caused more problems for our species, created more pain, produced more suffering, or resulted in more tragedy, than that which was intended to bring us our greatest joy—our relationships with each other. Neither individually nor collectively, socially nor politically, locally nor internationally, have we found a way to live in harmony. We simply find it very difficult to get along—much less actually love each other.

What's this all about? What's up here? I think I know. Not that I'm some kind of a genius, mind you, but I am a good listener. And I've been asking questions about this for a very long time. A few years ago, I began receiving answers. I believe those responses to have come from God. At the time I received them, I was so impacted and so impressed that I decided to keep a written record of what I was being given. That record became the *Conversations with God* series of books, which have become best-sellers around the world.

It is not necessary for you to join me in my belief about the source of my replies in order to receive benefit from them. All that is necessary is to remain open to the possibility that there just might be something that most humans do not fully understand about relationships, the understanding of which could change everything.

That's the frame of mind that a small group of about forty people held when it gathered at a home just outside San Francisco, California, in January 1999 to explore with me more deeply what *Conversations with God* has to say on this subject. I shared with the group all that I understood about the material on relationships that appears in the dialogue, and answered questions as they came up. The synergy of that afternoon produced an electrifying experience, resulting in an open flow of wonderful wisdom that, I am happy to say, was captured on videotape and audiocassette, edited versions of which have since been made public.

This book is a transcript of that event, and reads in a much more free-flowing—and, I think, more stimulating—style than text that is written for the printed page. And because the book format is not limited by time and production constraints, we were able to include here material not found in the video or audio versions, which necessarily had to be shortened for production reasons.

Essentially, what God tells us in *CWG* is that most of us enter into relationships for the wrong reasons. That is, for reasons having nothing to do with our overall purpose in life. When our reason for relationship is aligned with our soul's reason for being, not only are our relationships understood to be sacred, they are rendered joyful as well.

Joyful relationships. For far too many people, that phrase almost sounds like an oxymoron—a self-contradicting, mutually-exclusive term. Something like *military intelligence,* or *efficient government.* Yet it *is* possible to have joyful relationships, and the extraordinary insights in the *Conversations with God* books show us how.

Here are those insights as I have received them and understood them. I share them with you here in humility, straight from the Take It for What It's Worth Department, with the hope that if even one comment opens a new window or throws wide a doorway to greater happiness, you will have been served.

Neale Donald Walsch
July 1999
Ashland, Oregon

Relationships

Hello, everyone. Welcome to the room. Nice to see you all here.

The subject of the moment is human relationships, this thing with which some of us have so much difficulty. No one, I understand, in this room, but some of the rest of us have had some difficulty with this topic. And as you know, if you've read any of the writings that have come from my pen, I'm among those who have had some considerable difficulty in relationships—in making them work, and making them last, and, really, in causing them to even make any sense in my life.

I've never really understood, until these most recent days and times, what makes relationships work, and what their purpose is in my life. And the reason that was true for me is that, in the main, I found myself getting into relationships for all the wrong reasons.

By and large, I got *into* relationships with an eye toward what I could get *out* of them. And I'm not even sure I was willing to admit that to myself as I was getting into these relationships. I mean, I probably wouldn't have articulated it that way, because I didn't want myself to know myself. I wouldn't have said, "Gee, what is it I'm trying to get out of this?" I wouldn't have phrased it that way. I probably wouldn't even have conceptualized it in that way. But I noticed that's what I was up to, as soon as I stopped getting out of the relationship what I imagined that I would. In the moment that I stopped getting out of the relationship what I imagined that I would, *I* wanted to get out of the relationship.

And that's the pattern that I saw myself running through the largest portion of my adult life. I got out of relationships from which I did not get what I wanted. Did you follow that? And I got *into* relationships after I got out of other ones. Very quickly. So, I was a serial monogamist. Just one relationship after another, after another, after another, seeking and searching for that right and perfect mate who could, at last, fulfill me. Who could maybe see who I really am, and bring me to a place of happiness.

Now, I was willing to make a fair trade. It wasn't that I wasn't willing to show up in certain ways that could cause me to be attractive to another. Quite to the contrary, I knew how the game was played. And after a few failed relationships, I even began to know, or to think that I knew, what it was that others were looking for in a relationship. And so I worked very hard to provide that for them—as my negotiable goods, see. I learned, for instance, to sublimate certain parts of my own personality that I discovered, after a number of failed relationships, were not attractive to other people.

I'll give you one example, a silly one, but it's one that sticks with me because of its silliness, I think. I was with one lady for a while, and I thought she was going to be the love of my life. In fact, she *was* the love of my life during that time of my life I was with her. You know the old song, "When I am not near the one that I love, I love the one I'm near?" I know none of you have ever played that game.

So, I was in this particular relationship with this delicious lady. And I was deeply in love, or I thought that I was. And we went to the theater one night, in one of our early excursions into the outer world, the world of social stuff, you know. And so there I am at this play. And it was a comedy, and I began to laugh.

Now, I happen to have a very raucous, uproarious laugh. When I laugh, the whole room knows that I have laughed, unlike most of you, who aren't laughing very loudly at all, at any of this.

When I laugh, I really have this whole-feeling laughter. And it's just been part of me. I didn't design it that way; this is just how it is. Okay. So, here I am, and I'm roaring. Now, the players are, of course, loving it, because it's generating other laughter, and the room is becoming very alive. And so the actors are thrilled that in the audience they have what they call, as an actor, a live wire. "We've got a live wire in the house tonight."

So, I'm always welcome in places where there are performers, because I'm a real live wire. But the lady that I was with, and with whom I was so desperately in love (and I use that term advisedly—I was desperate *about* my love for her)—the more I laughed, the smaller she got. I can still see her to this day, sitting in the seat next to me, trying to disappear. And during intermission, she said, "Must you laugh like that?" And I remember thinking, "Like what?", because I wasn't even consciously aware, you know of what I was doing; that my laughter was causing her embarrassment. That it was, as we used to say as teenagers, spotting her out. That she felt somehow on the spot because of this guy she was with who was laughing in that way.

And I remember my deep desire to do whatever it took to keep her in the room. You know what I mean? I mean, figuratively, to keep her in the room of my life.

By the way, I should say, as an aside, I spent most of my life trying to keep you people in the room. I'll do anything. I'll do almost anything. Just stay in the room. Stay in the room. Don't leave the room. What can I do to keep you here? What part of my self can I set aside to keep you here? It's of no matter. I'll set it aside. All that matters is, stay in the room of my life.

And I can't tell you the number of tap dances that I did—and not even to my own music. You put the music on, and I'll dance the dance. And I did that this night at the theater.

Now comes act two, and I'm in the audience. And here come a few funny gag lines, and this is the action you're getting from Neale . . . ha . . . (sputtering) . . . sitting there trying to stifle my laugh. By act three, I had it down. By act three, I had turned "ha, ha, ha, ha" into "hee, hee . . ." And for several years, that's how I laughed. I used to laugh what I called a non-laugh, until somebody said, "Is something wrong with you? Are you okay?"

I was in a workshop with Dr. Elisabeth Kübler-Ross once, and she caught me at that. She called my number. She said something funny, and I was out there in the first row. She said, "What's the matter with you?"

"Nothing; I thought that was funny."

She said: "Why didn't you let that out?"

Anyone know Elisabeth Kübler-Ross? Very heavy Swiss accent. I became friends with her. I wound up working on her staff. Let that be a warning; some of you may be on my staff before the day is out.

And she said: "Why don't you let that out?" Or, in her Swiss accent, "Vy don't you let dat laughter out?"

And I said: "What do you mean? I was laughing."

She says: "No, you weren't. Why don't you let that laughter out? And while you're at it, why don't you let the pain out as well? The pain of holding in who you really are?"

So I was aware of what needed to be traded, or what I thought needed to be traded, to keep you in the room, you see. I was not unaware, and I was not unwilling. So, I did what I thought it took to keep the room filled. And that was the great puzzlement for me, because here I was doing what I thought it took to keep the room filled, and the room kept on emptying anyway. They kept on leaving anyway, until I finally found myself screaming: "What do you want? What does it take to make a relationship work?"

And I didn't even catch the act. I didn't even see that I was, in fact, trading this for that. I'll tell you what: I won't laugh like this if you don't cough like that. See, I won't eat like this, if you don't forget to put the toothpaste cap on the tube . . . like that, or whatever it is that we were trading. And the trades were much larger than that, I'm afraid.

And so, I wound up in this kind of a trade arrangement, you know. And on the 14th of February, I searched and searched for a card; but I couldn't find one that said, "I trade you very much. Gosh, do I trade you. And I'll trade you forever." But I was, in fact, playing trade. And again I knew that I was playing trade when the other person stopped trading me what I thought they were supposed to give me. That was our quid pro quo arrangement: I'll give you this, and you'll give me that. And when I stopped receiving what I thought I was supposed to receive, I left the relationship. Or, in some cases, when they stopped receiving what they thought was implicitly theirs, what they thought I was going to give them, they left the room.

And that's how I discovered that I was into relationships for all the wrong reasons, that I was somehow searching for that treasure, that negotiable currency that I could have which would be large enough to keep everyone in the room. What aspect of myself could be so attractive, so undeniable, so magnetic, that no matter what, you would stay in the room? And I didn't understand, until I had lost yet another in a series of important relationships, what was going wrong.

Then I had my extraordinary conversation with God, in which God said: "Neale, Neale, Neale, you clearly don't see what's going on here. First of all, you're in a relationship for all the wrong reasons. You're in relationship for what you can get out of it. And you're willing to trade all right. But you see it as just that—almost a business transaction. And you don't understand the purpose of a relationship. And the purpose of a relationship has nothing to do with what you think you can get out of it, and everything to do with what you choose to put into it. But not putting something into it as a *means of extracting from it what you wish to receive*, but simply putting something into it as a means of noticing who you really are.

"So, what you put into a relationship, be sure that you put into it authentically. And never deny, for one moment, the real you. And if the real you isn't sufficient or attractive enough to keep that person in the room, then let them leave. Because someone will come into the room of your life who will find the authentic you attractive enough. And when they come into the room out of their response to your authenticity, they will stay because you don't have to keep your act going in order to keep them in the room, you see. And so the tap dance can be over."

And that changed everything for me in relationships. It shifted the whole paradigm of my experience, because at last I understood what I was doing there.

I also understood that relationship is the most important single experience we could possibly create for ourselves. And that in the absence of relationship, we are nothing. Without you, I am nothing at all. You probably knew that when you walked in. You sat down; "Without me, Neale's nothing." (laughter) But it's true. Because without you, I'm nothing at all.

[Pointing to different people] And without you, I'm nothing. And without you, I'm nothing at all. And that is true, because absent the experience of relationship, we are not. In this relative experience, I can only be who I am in relationship to something else in my experience. I mean, experientially, I can't know a thing about myself unless you're in the room.

And I was given an interesting illustration by God that allowed me to notice how this could be true. God said to me: "Imagine that you are in an all-white room, totally white: white floor, white ceiling, white walls. And imagine you are suspended in that room, as if by magic, so that you couldn't touch anything, just dangling there, like a Christmas ornament, without even a string attaching you to it, just suspended in mid-air. Here you are in this sea of whiteness. And imagine that nothing else exists at all. How long do you think that you will exist in your own experience?" And the answer came up for me: "Probably not terribly long, not very long."

Because, in the absence of anything else, I am not. Not in my own experience. I mean, I am that I am. But I can't *know* that I am. I can't experience that I am, except in relationship to something else. So, I can't know anything about myself.

Yet, if somebody were to walk into that room of whiteness, and just put so much as the tiniest speck of ink on the wall, to the degree that I could see that speck of ink, that little black dot, to that degree suddenly I exist. First of all, "over there" would exist, and "over here". Because the dot would be there, and I would be here. I would begin to define myself in relationship to that other thing. In this case, the dot on the wall. I would imagine that I am the thing called . . . Maybe I would utter a word that sounded like "big-g-ger".

I might even have the audacity to say, with regard to the dot on the wall, that I'm "sma-a-arter". Sometimes I don't think that I'm very much smarter than the dot on the wall, but, generally speaking, I imagine that I am. I may be faster, or slower, or "this-er", or "that-er", you understand, in relationship to the dot.

Put a cat in the room, and suddenly I have much larger experiences of myself, because that which is also in the space is much larger than the dot on the wall. So now I begin to conceptualize all kinds of things about me. Maybe the cat is softer than I am, but maybe I am older than the cat, or whatever. You see, I start conceiving of myself in my own experience, based on who and what is around me. Therefore, relationship—I'm talking now in the realm of the relative, in which we exist in physical form—relationship with other people, places, and things is not only important, it is vital. And in the absence of our relationship with everything, we are not.

And so I begin to understand the reason that relationship exists at all—my relationship with this table, with this glass of water, and with those of you who share this time and place with me. And it is out of my relationship with you that I not only know myself—here comes the trick—not only do I know myself out of my relationship with you, but I literally *define* myself as well. That is to say: I define and, in that sense, *re-create who I am* in relationship to who you are.

Here comes an interesting twist. Ultimately, I cannot re-create myself as anything that you are not. That is to say: I can only see in me what I'm willing to see in you. And that which I fail to see in you, I will never find in myself, because I don't know that it exists. Therefore, I cannot find the divinity within me until I seek, discover, and recognize (that is to say: know again, to re-*cognize*) the divinity in you. And to the degree that I fail to recognize and to know the divinity in you, to that degree I cannot know it in me, nor can I know any good thing about myself. Nor any bad thing either, for that matter. For nothing can exist over here that does not exist over there. And the reasons for that are multitudinous; not the least of which is, there is only one of us in the room.

There's no one else here. So, we find that relationship has a unique place in our life, not just an important place—if I can use a twist of words—an irreplaceable place. I mean, you can't replace it. There's nothing that you can replace relationship with that will bring you what relationship brings you, because relationship is the only experience in life that brings you an experience of yourself in life. And we are talking here about not only your relationship to people, but also to places, and things, and even events—even your relationship to the occurrences of your life.

We all have a relationship to the circumstances and the events of our lives. And it is out of our relationship, which is entirely self-created, that we experience, announce, and declare, express, fulfill, and become, who we really are.

Once we understand the sacred place that relationship holds in the experience of all of us, we hold the experience of relationship as sacred in deed—not just in thought, not just in word, but in *deed*. And the deeds we do around relationships begin to change dramatically.

First we see the secret that I announced a moment ago: that only what I see in you can I see in me. And so it becomes our primary function in relationship, once this secret is understood, to look deeply at you, to see in you the grandest vision I could ever imagine; indeed, even to assist you in creating that, to the degree that you choose to avoid creating it. So one thing that partners do with and for each other is not seek to take from another, but to seek to give to another, and to empower that other with whom you are partnered to express and experience who they really are, because we see the vital importance of that. And we see that that is, in fact, the *raison d'être* of all relationships, their very reason for being.

Suddenly our purpose in a relationship becomes entirely transmuted and transformed. We are no longer trying to find out what we can get from the relationship, but what can we give. What can we empower? What can we create?

What can we cause to be realized, made real—be *real*-ized? You know, how you "simonize" your car? You can "realize" people. You just shine them up a bit. And they become *real*-ized. And this, in the end, is the ultimate of self-realization.

And that's the secret I want to share with you today. Many people are involved in the self-realization movement. And they think that self-realization is somehow achieved by sitting quietly by yourself. Because, after all, it's called self-realization. So, we're going to realize ourselves by sitting quietly by ourselves alone in a room, with a candle perhaps, and maybe some quiet music. And maybe we make some interesting sounds, you know, "Ohhhmmm." Whatever we do, and I'm not putting that down, I'm not making that wrong, but if you think that that is the way to self-realize, and that the more hours you spend doing that . . . you will not have understood the grand wisdom: that we are here for each other.

Ultimately, self-realization is not achieved alone. Self-realization is achieved when we realize the Self as seen in another. That is why all true masters do nothing but walk around, giving other people back to themselves. Have you ever been seen by a living master? Have you ever been in the presence of someone that you considered a spiritual master, or as close to it as we're going to get in this lifetime? Have you been in the room with someone who is working toward that level of self-mastery? If you have (and you'll recognize them at once), you will notice that they spend the majority of their days and times seeing mastery in you. They will look at you, look in your eyes, and see you as even you do not imagine yourself to be. And you'll wonder, why *you* don't see you as they see you? Then *they* will wonder why you don't see you. I'll try that again. (laugh) This is obviously a statement I'm not supposed to make. Are we all ready to be quiet? Then they will wonder why they do not . . . and they will wonder why you do not . . . Forget it . . . . (laughs) I know when the elements have defeated me.

When we use a relationship in this delicious way, we transform our whole experience of ourselves with our loved ones. Suddenly, we want nothing *from* them—and only want to give everything *to* them. And we seek to give everything we are to them, needing nothing in return.

Now, be clear. This doesn't mean we allow them to walk all over us. This doesn't mean we allow ourselves to be somehow the victims in a relationship that's dysfunctional with them. That's not what we're talking about here. Life does not require us to stay in the same room with someone who is abusing us. And that's why I'm leaving this room right now. You could laugh a little more loudly at my jokes . . . .

But it does mean that as we give of ourselves to others in the fullest measure, we allow ourselves the experience of a love that knows no condition, even as we say, "I choose not to co-reside with you." See, one of these days we'll even find a way to do the thing called separate from each other without bitterness. See, we won't need attorneys. You know the only reason we need lawyers? Because there are lawyers.

One of these days we'll be able to look at each other and say: "I notice now that our time together is concluded. I notice now that it's the moment for us to continue to love each other without condition, to continue to give each other the gifts that are ours to give in fullness, and yet, to do so from across the room, or across the street, or from around the world. Because certain of your physical behaviors are not in harmony with how I choose to live my life. And that doesn't mean that I don't love you."

One of these days, we'll be able to speak that truth without having to somehow find something wrong with the other, or make them the villain of the piece in order to justify our truth. When we can get to that place, we can also create, then, the loving, enduring relationships that we long for in our lives, because those relationships, too, are suddenly hinged on no condition whatsoever, and no limitation, either.

Here's what I know about the best relationships, and how they work. First of all, they are relationships that know no condition. There is no conditionality to the best relationships. There is no limitation. Because relationships that are based in real love—a love that is true—are relationships that are totally and completely free.

Freedom is the essence of who you are. Freedom is the essence of love. The word *love* and the word *freedom* are interchangeable. As is the word *joy*. Joy, love, freedom—love, freedom, love, joy. They all mean the same thing. And the human soul cannot be joyful to the degree that it's restricted or limited in any way.

Therefore, when we love another, we never ever seek to limit or restrict them in any way whatsoever. Love says, "My will for you is your will for you." Love says, "I choose for you what you choose for you." When I say, "I choose for you what *I* choose for you," then I'm not loving you. I'm loving me *through* you, because I'm getting what I want, rather than seeing you get what you want.

Here is the supreme irony of that paradigm: The moment that I say, "I choose for you what you choose for you," you will never leave me. Because all we are searching for is someone who will let us have what we want out of life. See, the whole world contrives to not let us have what we want out of life, starting with our parents, at the age of two. "No, you can't have that." It went on to our teachers in school. "Do not chew gum in class." And much larger restrictions, thank you very much.

It continued through our adolescent years, when our budding sexuality caused us to want one thing, and the world contrived to demonstrate to us that it was somehow inappropriate to want that—in some religions, to even desire it. Oh, what havoc we have wreaked on this planet with our insane sexual stuff. Insanity.

And it continued in our young-adult years, and even into the later days of our adulthood, with the world contriving to tell us we cannot have what we really want. I mean, I even know some wives who actually go to some husbands, and say: "Honey, there's a quilting class down at the Y. It's every Tuesday night for six weeks. I'd like to take it." And I actually know some husbands who say, "No." Can you imagine a husband saying to a wife, "I don't want you taking that quilting class"? Yet, it happens.

"Archie. It's just a quilting class, Arch."

"Stifle it. Stifle yourself, Edith."

Remember that? And the reason that the whole country laughed at Archie Bunker was that half the country saw itself there. And it was an embarrassed laugh.

I had a father—God rest his soul—and I love him dearly, but he was very, very much like that. He wasn't quite Archie Bunker-ish in some ways; he didn't have those racial ideas, or thoughts, but, boy, did he have the thoughts: "I'm the ruler of the house. And she can't take a quilting class without my permission, and I will rarely give it."

In a relationship that is constructed around a genuine expression of real love, not only is it okay if the wife comes to the husband and says, "Can I take a quilting class?" it's also okay if the wife comes to the husband and says: "Can I have lunch with Harry? And by the way, my darling, your name is not Harry." And the husband, we'll call him Mike, says: "My will for you is your will for you. You want to have lunch with Harry? Have lunch with Harry. I love you enough to want for you what you want for you."

If Harry has any thought of somehow stealing that person from Mike, he might as well forget it, because the number of people who are going to leave the Mikes, who give them that kind of freedom to express themselves, is minuscule. But huge is the number of women who will walk away from Mike immediately if Mike says: "You can't have lunch with Harry—in fact, don't even mention his name in this house!

Don't even think about it—what's the matter with you anyway? Don't you realize that you belong to me? You're my woman."

Women do this to men, too, incidentally. "By the way, sweetheart, I'd like to have lunch with Matilda." "I don't think so." I use a silly, way-out example to make a point. Life will bring you these opportunities to demonstrate who you really are, in large quantities.

Love never says no. You know how I know that? Because God never says no. And God and love are interchangeable. God would never say no to you, no matter what your request. Even if God thought that what you're asking for is going to get you into trouble. Like Matilda. Or Harry. Or anything else. See, God will never say no, because God realizes that ultimately you can't get into the biggest trouble. That is to say, you can't damage yourself in a way that causes you not to be. You can only evolve and grow, and become more of who you really are. So, God says to us: "I choose for you what you choose for you. And I dare you to do that with those whom *you* love."

Now, wake up. I want you all to wake up. Because I want you to know, you'll start falling asleep as soon as you are confronted with that which you do not want to hear. You'll literally start falling asleep right in your chair. (laugh) And you'll think, of course, that it's to do with something else other than what he's talking about. "I'm just tired." That is the mechanism of the subconscious, when it starts confronting data that it does not want to fully receive or embrace. "I'll just sleep through this part." Be careful, because most of us are sleepwalking through life. So, be careful you don't spend your life sleepwalking. Stay awake. Stay awake. You do not know the hour that your master will come.

There's a question in the audience on this delicate subject of relationship. Let us see what that question is . . . .

Neale, in Book 3 *of* Conversations with God, *you asked God about the institution of marriage. And . . . God nixed it, said that it didn't have a lot of validity. Do you believe that?*

Well, I think you misread what God had to say there. God did not say that marriage has no validity, and God did not nix it. God said that marriage, the way you are currently constructing it—

The institution.

Well, even the institution, *the way you've currently devised it*—not the institution per se, and not marriage per se, but marriage the way you [society] have constructed it, the way you have devised it—has no validity, given where you say you want to go.

Validity itself is a relative term. Relative to what? Valid relative to what? See, God says there's no such thing as right or wrong, believe it or not, because right and wrong are relative terms. A thing that is right yesterday is wrong today, and vice versa. And life has demonstrated that to us amply.

We don't need to go into that here. Any thinking person understands that right and wrong are relative terms. And God uses the terms right and wrong, or valid or invalid, relative to what we are announcing and declaring that we are choosing for ourselves, as a species and as individuals.

We have announced and declared that we choose for ourselves for marriage to be the highest expression of the grandest experience of love of which humans are capable. That's what we've said. We have said, "We choose for marriage to be an expression of the grandest and highest love of which humans are capable." Then we proceed to construct a marriage institution and a marriage experience that produces exactly the opposite of that—virtually the lowest form of love of which humans are capable. A love that possesses, rather than releases. A love that limits, rather than expands. A love that owns, rather than disowns. A love that makes virtually everything around it smaller, rather than making everything around it larger.

We've created an experience of marriage that has nothing to do with love, in far too many instances. We've created a holder, a shell, some kind of an encasement. And that's what we want marriage to be. We want it to be an encasement that holds everything exactly where it was the moment you said I love you, and that holds everyone exactly where they were in that first moment. But people and events move around. They change. Life is an evolution. And so marriage, as we have constructed it, works against the very process of life itself, because it provides very little breathing room in the way many societies and religions and family traditions have constructed it.

Largely, marriage has been used by those societies, religions, and families as a mini-prison, as kind of a contractual arrangement that says: "Everything will be, now and forevermore, the way it is in just this moment. You will love no one else, and you certainly won't demonstrate that love for anyone else in the way you demon-strate your love for me. You won't go anywhere else except where I go. You'll do very little that I do not do with you, and in most ways from this day forward your life is going to be, at least to some degree, limited." And so the very thing that should unlimit people and release the spirit within them, works against that, and limits people and closes that spirit down.

That's the irony of marriage as we've cre-ated it. We say "I do," and from the moment we say "I do," we *can't* do the things that we would really love to do in life, in largest measure. Now very few people would admit this in the first throes of romance and in the first moments af-ter their marriage. They would only come to these conclusions three, or five . . . or, what's the famous phrase, "the seven-year itch" . . . seven years later, when they suddenly realize that, in fact, their experience of themselves in the world at large has been reduced, and *not* en-larged, by the institution of marriage.

That's not true, of course, in all marriages, naturally. But it's true in enough of them. I'm going to say, in the majority of them. And that is why we have such a high divorce rate, because it isn't so much that people have gotten tired of each *other*, not nearly so often as they've gotten tired of the *restrictions* and the *limitations* that marriage seems to have imposed upon them. The human heart knows when it's being asked to be less.

Now love, on the other hand, is all about freedom. The very definition of love is freedom itself. Love is that which is free, and knows no limitation, restriction, or condition of any kind. And so I think that what we have done here is that we have created an artificial construction around that which is least artificial. Love is the most authentic experience within the framework of the human adventure. And yet in the midst of this grand authenticity, we have created these artificial constrictions. And that makes it very difficult for people to stay in love.

And so what we have to do is reconstruct marriage, if we're going to have marriage at all, in a way that says: "I do not limit you. There is no condition that makes it okay for us to remain together. I do not have any desire to cause you to be less in your expression of yourself, in any way. Indeed, what this marriage is intended to do, this new form of marriage, is to fuel the engine of your experience—the experience of who you really are and who you chose to be."

And one last thing that the New Marriage does: It says, "I recognize that even you, yourself, will change. Your ideas will change, your tastes will change, your desires will change. Your whole understanding of who you are had *better* change, because if it doesn't change, you've become a very static personality over a great many years, and nothing would displease me more. And so I recognize that the process of evolution will produce changes in you."

This new form of marriage not only allows for such changes, but it encourages them.

Your old construction of the institution of marriage, given what you say you want to do and what you want it to be, is invalid. That is not a valid way to produce that. And yet, we're still trying to produce that in our daily lives, with the old way we have constructed marriages.

Even the marriage vows, some of the traditional marriage vows (thanks goodness we've changed a few of them through the years), but even some of the marriage vows, for centuries, talked in terms of ownership, and created philosophical constructions that couldn't possibly support what true love would choose to create.

And young people, by the way, know this. Young people know this instinctively, which is why, for years, and increasingly in the sixties, seventies, and eighties, young people would look at older people and say: "You know, we're not buying it. We're not doing it. We're not going there."

And so they did this thing called living together, which, of course, in the sixties and seventies was like "How can they do that?" In the late fifties, in 1958, if you lived with someone, it was a scandal. But soon, kids were doing it right and left, saying: "You know, you can take your idea of marriage and toss it, because we don't get it. We get that love does not limit, does not own, does not hold in, but expands, lets go, and releases, the grandest part of who all of us are."

And so, as has been the case really from the beginning of time, whenever any major change had been made in society, it was the babes among us, the children among us, who showed us. It was not us old fuddy-duddies with all this gray in our hair, but it was, by and large, the young among us who said: "We know, and we can show you, a better way. And now we're going to do that."

As we see this huge shift into the twenty-first century, we notice that not only are—this is really the funny part—not only are the young people, the teenagers and the just-after-teenagers, living together, but so, too, are older folks. The 80-, and 70-, and 65-year-olds are looking at each other, going: "Well, Martha, they're doing it. Why don't we do it? Let's just live together." And a shocking number of 65- and 70-, and 80-year-old women are actually saying, "Well, why not?"

Now, this is not an argument against marriage as an institution. Let's be clear. This is an exploration of what we've created the institution of marriage to be in the largest number of cases. There are many marriages that are created in such a loving way, that there's no sense of conditionality or limitation to them. I'm happy to say that my wife and I have such a relationship, as an example. And that's the reason that it's the best relationship of my life. Because my wife and I don't know of limitation, and we will not allow our love to be conditioned by any particular response or set of responses, or any particular behavior, but rather there is only one behavior that Nancy and I require of each other: "*Live authentically*. Live your truth. And if you love me for anything, love me because I live mine." Can you hear that? That's when you know you're in a blesséd relationship.

I once turned to Nancy after being with her about three years, and I said something that I was struck with after I said it. I looked at her quite spontaneously one day and said, "You know, living with you is like living alone." That's a grand thing to say. Because I am most authentic, you know, most myself, when there's no one else around. I might get out of bed and walk around naked for a whole ten minutes. I may even sneak down to the kitchen with no clothes on, or jump into the pool. I may say certain things; I may sing a song; I may . . . I may just do stuff, just *be* in ways that I have this imagined idea that I can only be and do when I'm totally alone. Except now I'm with this delicious person, and being with her is like being alone.

She has given me back to myself, and said, "You know how I love you most?"

I say, "No. How?"

And she says, "Just the way you're showing up now."

"You mean, overweight and all? Big laugh and all?"

"I not only love you in spite of your laughter, I love you because of it. I not only love you in spite of what you imagine your faults to be, I love you because of them."

That's love. Everything else is counterfeit.

By the way, do you know what faults are? (I left my handkerchief somewhere else, and I can't even cry now at my own material.) Do you know what faults are? (Someone hands him a tissue.) Thank you very much. False evidence appearing real, for sure. But that's fear—false evidence appearing real. I used to think that I was a person with all these faults, and that's why I couldn't make relationships work.

I used to think, if only I straightened myself out, then I could present myself in a package that you would endure, if not enjoy. Because I thought that I had all these faults, because all these people in my life, including (God bless them) my parents some of the time, were telling me about all the faults that I had, you know. And then I ran across a teacher a number of years ago who made something astonishingly clear to me. She said, "Consider the possibility that your biggest faults are your grandest assets, simply with the volume turned up just a tiny bit too high. Consider the possibility that the very thing people fell in love with you because of, is what sometimes turns them away from you as well, because you've tweaked the volume just a little bit. And so, what maybe your friends call your unbearable braggadocio, when they say, 'He's just too too much,' is the same thing, the exact same quality, they look for, when it's 'who can lead the pack, who can get us out of this mess? Neale's the leader in the room. He's the one. That's why we like you so much, Neale.'"

I'm a very spontaneous person. So when people want somebody spontaneous, who can dream up something just that quickly and pop it into the room just that fast . . . "Hey, Neale's the one."

That's also the part of me they say is (all together now), "irresponsible." So, my irresponsibility is just my spontaneity turned up just one or two notches too loud. And so, what this teacher said was: "Neale, it's just a question of the volume sometimes being just a little bit off. But don't erase that. Don't try to change that about yourself. Don't try to eliminate that aspect of who you are from your behavior. Don't disown that. Just turn the volume down, ever so little, and notice that there's an appropriate volume to the aspects of who you are that renders itself acceptable in every moment. And sometimes you'll have to turn that volume up, and sometimes you'll have to turn that volume down."

Isn't that a delicious way to think of it? So now I don't have to think that I'm this person with all these faults. I simply have all these great qualities, sometimes turned up a little bit too much. (But not often—anymore.) Got it?

So, true relationship sees and knows all of this. True relationship is *foundationed,* or built upon, an entirely new paradigm that says: "I see in you what I choose to see in me. I give to you what I choose, myself, to receive." And true relationship also says: "What I take from you, or seek to disallow you to have, I take from me. I cannot allow myself to have what I will not allow you to have."

And so our challenge is: Can we live in a relationship without condition? Can we live in a relationship that doesn't ever say no, but simply says yes to another? Can we use relationship as an expression of the grandest kind of love we could ever imagine? Do we love our loved one enough to say the three magic words? Not "I love you." They're, quite frankly, a bit over-used. But here are the three magic words of every relationship: *As you wish.*

As *you* wish.

When we're prepared to say that, then we have truly given people back to themselves. Until we're ready to say that, we have simply sought to use our relationship with another to bring to us what we imagine ourselves to need in order to be happy. You have a question . . .

Well, there are, you know, a million questions. But this is a subject that I have made my life about. I have been teaching courses on relationship for many years now. I'm in a long-term marriage. I have lived what you're speaking successfully for many years. And in the moment, I am not living it successfully. So, I would say that I've really done laps with this. And I have a marriage that has enormous freedom in it. And it has been a marriage that's been grounded on a declaration I made when I began it, which was: Our relationship works; it makes a difference, and everything contributes. So, I lived from the space that whatever was happening didn't need to match my pictures; anything that was going on was a part of how it was serving me. And it was, in fact, working, even when it didn't look the way

I wanted it to. I saw that my ability to work with the challenges of it was how I could contribute to the world.

So, what's the problem?

Well, the problem is that somehow we are stuck in a power struggle that we are not moving through. And I cannot see how to move through it. So, I don't know what to ask. I just know that I do deeply love my husband. He deeply loves me on an essence level—

So, I understand that you're in this power struggle. Now, I want to say to you with regard to that, something that may sound a bit heartless almost. "So what?" Why is that not okay with you? Why is the condition called "being in a power struggle" not okay with you? What's not all right about that?

I am basing a lot of my current dissatisfaction on what I'm not getting from the relationship. So, that conversation about not wanting to get anything from the relationship, and only looking at what I want to put into the relationship, is the seed I'm walking away with so far this morning. I hear what you're saying. There is a lack of the experience of love in the relationship. On an essence level, there's deep love. And when we surrender, there are many times we will almost step outside of our human identities, be with each other, and I feel like we finally have gotten out of the boxing ring. We're like the two boxers—when they ring the bell, they hang on to each other. There's that moment of love, because we do love each other deeply. And I am his equal, and he is my equal. And so we are enormously equal in the power struggle, and it wipes you out. And when there's this moment of not being in that struggle, there's a recognition of partnership and love, and the transcendent bondedness that's there. And in the everyday process of living, we are hurting each other a lot.

Well, stop it.

How do I do that without just adapting to conditions that really don't work for me?

Don't adapt to conditions that are not working for you. Simply stop making an issue over the fact that you refuse to adapt. Just don't adapt. For instance, I'm going to use a simple example. Let's say that someone decides . . . Let's say that Nancy decided to take up smoking. Nancy currently doesn't smoke, and neither do I, but I'm going to use a real easy example we can all kind of just "get."

Okay, that'd be great.

So, now Nancy comes home with a package of cigarettes, and decides: "Oh . . . I thought I'd tell you. I'm going to smoke." Well, I might have a problem with that. Not a problem with Nancy per se, because Nancy's still Nancy. But now she's Nancy the Smoker. And I might have difficulty adapting to that behavior.

Well, I can simply refuse to adapt to that behavior. But I can do so without making Nancy wrong, without making an issue of the fact that I'm not adapting to the behavior, without causing my refusal to adapt to that be-havior to come between us. I can simply say to Nancy: "Gosh, I love you, now as I always have. And it doesn't work for me for you to smoke in my presence. So I'm going to leave the room now. Enjoy your cigarette. Incidentally, since you insist on smoking in the house continually, I'll probably have to leave the house, because I don't like to be in a home that's filled with ciga-rette smoke. And I love you. I love you as dearly as I ever did, and I'm leaving the house now. And I love you."

Now Nancy might say, if she were not very evolved (which she is), but if she weren't, she might say: "You mean you're leaving the house just because I'm smoking. And you're trying to tell me you're not making me wrong." And I would say: "I understand that you may have the need to tell me that I am making you wrong, but I'm simply allowing myself to live my authentic truth. I love you, and I notice you're smoking now. And what works for me is to be in a home that's smoke-free. So if you continue to smoke

in this home, I'm going to have to live somewhere else. And I'm going to have to love you
from somewhere else."

Okay. I get that.

The issues over which people traditionally
enter into power struggles generally have to do
with issues of time and availability and the activities of the other. In other words, you're not
spending enough time with me, or you're en-
gaged in activities with which I disagree. And
we are at struggle about those issues. Now, I'll
give you an example of what that could look
like in real life: Suddenly your spouse turns into
a workaholic, and while they were spending a
lot of time with you in the first three years of
your marriage, suddenly they're spending less
and less, and now you're seven or eight or ten
years into it, and they're hardly spending any
time with you at all. And you enter into a power
struggle over this, because you are trying to
control their time.

And so you say to them: "You know, I want you home here, at least three weekends out of four. I don't want you on the road all the time, or always on location shooting some great big film or doing some great big project, or poring over your work, or handling whatever it is that you're doing. You're not paying any attention to me." They wouldn't say it in those exact words, perhaps—maybe some who are very, very frank would—but most people would couch it in different terms. They wouldn't just come right out and say, "The truth is, I want your attention. I want your time." And so, there's a power struggle.

Maybe the partner will try to make an uneasy bargain: "Okay, I'll only go out on the road one weekend a month, or two weekends a month." They'll strike an agreement, and then if they decide to spend three weekends in a particular month away, they start feeling guilty, they start feeling henpecked, then they start feeling *controlled*, and resentment builds up and pretty soon you have a power struggle:

"What right do you have to tell me what to do with my time?"

I would never enter into that kind of a power struggle with my spouse. If my spouse were doing anything, anything at all, with which I disagreed, or that didn't work for me, I would simply say: "You know, you can do as you wish. And I have to tell you that it doesn't feel good over here for you to spend three weekends out of four away from me, and away from this home. And it's okay if you want to do that, but I want you to know what I'm going to do if you continue that over a long period. I'm going to find someone else to spend my weekends with.

"That isn't a threat. I'm not trying to hammer you with this. It's simply an announcement of what works for me. I'd like to be with someone. I like to share the days and times of my life with a beloved other, and it's all right if you don't choose to be that beloved other. And so, you just do as you wish and as you please. And, no resentment, there's no anger, there's no upset, there's no make-wrong. Just a simple statement of fact. Now let me close my discussion with you with the following statement of fact: If I could choose anyone to be my beloved other, it would be you. That's why I'm wearing this ring on my finger. You don't have to make the same choice in this moment, but I want you to know that you are my first choice, but also that I *do have a second*, and a third, and a fourth."

Now, there's simply a transfer of information, and even that transfer of information is not done belligerently. It's not about "I gotcha." It's just about, "this is what is so. This is simply what's so. And I share it with you lovingly, and openly and candidly, as people who say they are in love with each other ought to do. This is my open, candid truth. And that's what so about that. And now we all have the facts, and we all can make informed choices."

What I'm saying is not that I have someone in the wings ready to jump in here if you make one minor misstep, so you'd better watch your p's and q's; but what I am saying here is, if in the long run you choose to exhibit a behavior that is not working for me, that is simply not functional in my life—oh, and by the way, if I should choose in the long run to repeatedly exhibit a behavior that's not functional in *yours*—that there are options. I'm not limited to simply responding to that behavior by accepting it. I don't have to do that. And I just want you to know openly and candidly that, should you choose over the long run to exhibit that behavior, I will probably have to make some adjustments in how I'm proceeding with my life. And those adjustments might, in fact, include inviting someone else to provide for me, and to share with me many of the things that I had hoped I'd be sharing with you.

You see, there's no power struggle when there's no struggle over power. There's simply each person—or at least one of the two (because it takes two to tango)—there's simply each person removing themselves from the struggle, and returning to the place of their own power, by allowing themselves to be, do, and have what they choose, without making the other wrong about it.

"Choose what you're choosing. Choose to smoke. Choose whatever you're choosing, and I'll choose what I'm choosing." Now that allows Nancy to make a value judgment. Is smoking important enough to her to allow her relationship with me to be changed in such a way that I'm no longer in the room? Or, for that matter, no longer even sharing the same house? And she'll make that value judgment. She'll either continue to smoke, and demonstrate that smoking is, in fact, important enough to her to allow her relationship with me to change in such a way, or she will stop smoking. She'll alter her behavior. Not because I'm making her, but because she has made a *free-will, empowered choice* to notice that she can control the outcomes of her life by controlling her behaviors. See the difference?

I got it. Thank you.

You're very welcome. But that's how love reacts. Love does not struggle with power. Never.

Yes, another question . . .

Neale, what is your own greatest challenge in relationship?

My own greatest challenge in relationship is transparency—remaining visible. Even after a number of years now with the same wonderful mate, there's always that little moment of fear. What if she finds out about this? What if she finds out about that . . . she won't love me any more; you know, if she knows that I took that five thousand and invested into a stock and I lost it, and I never told her about that; or that I actually went out one afternoon and bought a car.

That was the big thing I did two years ago. I was driving down the road and I turned into a car lot—a new car lot. And I saw a car that I really, really wanted. And I said, "I'll take it." Just like that, I bought a car in twenty minutes. And I just drove it home. And then I thought all the way home, "This is ridiculous." I'm driving home thinking, "How can I hide this car from my wife?" I knew she had to find out sooner or later. Probably before dinner; you know, "Whose car is in the driveway?" But I actually was thinking (I went back to the sixth grade), "How can I prolong her not knowing?" Then I thought, "You know, this is crazy." I got on the cell phone while I was driving and said, "Be outside when I pull up, I've got something to show you." And she said, "What are you talking about?" And I said, "I just bought a car." (Gulp)

So I think transparency is my greatest challenge in relationship, even with somebody who I trust with my life. I mean, I really trust Nancy with my life. I trust the unconditionality of her love. And still I worry about being totally clear and totally open and completely honest with her about every feeling, every thought, every idea, every understanding and misunderstanding, and every single thing that I'm doing, you know? And I'll tell you where that comes from, I think. I think my fear of transparency in relationship goes back to an age-old, ancient fear of God. Of course my idea was that God is going to "get me" for this.

By the way, I should tell you I still have that idea to this very day. At some small level, there's still a tiny part of my being—in spite of what's come through me, in spite of what's been written in the astonishing *Conversations with God* books—there are still some nights I roll around on the pillow, "Oh, man, what if I'm making this all up? I mean, what if I'm wrong about all of this? What if I've misled millions of people—about God? Boy, if I'm wrong, God is gonna get me good."

Then I have to become transparent with God, and say: "You know God, if I am wrong, I trust you'll know I didn't mean it. I mean, I didn't mean to intentionally mislead anyone. And if there's a shred of mercy left in You, gimme a break on this one."

You understand? Now that isn't at all the God that I know really exists. That's the God of my imagination, the God of my fear. And I think that the deep fear we have that we're going to be judged and misunderstood and punished by Deity is transferred to other people in our lives: to our spouse, to our loved ones, to our boss at work, to people who hold some place of importance in our life. And so, my biggest challenge in relationship is to think of those people who are important to me in relationship as I now want to think of God: as my best friend. I want to have a friendship with God, and I want to have a friendship with my spouse and all of my loved ones, of such quality that I can stand naked before them, mentally as well as physically, and say: "This is it—there's nothing hidden, there are no hidden agendas. This is *all* of it." That's my biggest challenge, and I face that challenge every day.

> *I want to ask you, just briefly, Neale, about mirroring in relationship—that*

what you dislike in the person you're with, you actually dislike in yourself. Could you just comment briefly on that?

You know, I don't dislike very much in other people any more, because I learned long ago that what I saw over there that I disliked was merely something that I saw over here that I disliked. And in recent years I've come to like everything about me. Isn't that amazing? I mean, it's kind of hard to believe when you sit here and look at me, I suppose, but I really like so much about me now. I like my appearance. I like my attitudes. I like my ideas. I like my wackiness. I like my spontaneity. I like the part of me that's totally unconventional. I like the part that's not okay. You know, I even like my laugh. I mean, I like everything about me, and I have to tell you it's the first time in my life that I have felt that way. And because I feel that way, there's very little about other people now that I don't like. I've become tremendously tolerant. It's extraordinary that I look at people all around me, and I just love them all. I find acceptable, behaviors and characteristics and personality traits that even a few years ago I would have rejected out of hand. So I think that what happens is that with self-love comes an enormous love for other people, because I have to think to myself, "Gosh, you know, if you can love yourself, you can love anything."

What are the five levels of truth telling?

When I talk about transparency in relationship, I often think of telling the truth, which is what transparency really is all about. And I've been made aware that there are really five levels of truth telling.

The first level of truth telling is when you tell the truth to yourself about yourself. That was an enormous challenge for me, because I had been lying to myself for many, many years. It's hard to think of a person literally lying to themselves, but it's easy to do, and I did it for a long time.

The second level of truth telling is when you tell the truth to yourself about another. And I lied to myself about those kinds of things, as well, for many, many years. For instance, as an example, for years I told myself that I loved, in a romantic way, a person that I was with. Whenever I thought that I didn't, whenever I allowed myself to even imagine, "You know, maybe I'm not in love with her any more," a voice inside my head said, "Don't be silly, of course you love her." Because that's what I was *supposed* to be thinking. That's how it was *supposed* to be for me. And so, I just lied to myself about that for the longest time, until one day I told the truth to myself about another. Didn't even utter it out loud, just told it to myself, which was a huge hurdle.

Then the third level of truth telling is when I tell the truth about myself *to* another, much as I'm doing with you right now.

And the fourth level of truth telling is when I tell the truth about another, *to that other*—my truth, of course, not *the* truth. *The* truth, objectively, doesn't exist, but I share my inner-most truth about another, with that other.

And the fifth level of truth telling, when you get there, is when you tell the truth to everyone about everything. And if you can take these five steps, you've taken five steps to heaven, because heaven (pause) is not having to lie any more.

> *I've heard it said that sometimes it seems that pain makes the heart break open so that it can experience more love. Why do our hearts sometimes need to be broken open, in order to feel?*

I don't think they do. Whoever said that pain makes the heart break open so it can experience more love maybe described a phenomenon that happens, but not one that *has* to happen. I think it's entirely possible to experience and feel more love without any pain at all. But we live our own cultural myth. There's a huge cultural myth out there that says that love hurts and that pain is the avenue; you know, no pain, no gain, that whole thing. I have to tell you I'm discovering and have been discovering now for the past several years, that it's possible to love joyously, and to feel all the love that the human heart can hold and more, without any pain whatsoever. So I'm ready now to say that I can reject out of hand the notion that pain and love have to go hand in hand, and that there's only one way to get from here to there, and that's through the doorway marked "pain." It's not necessary; it is a cultural myth, and we can step aside from it quite arbitrarily by simply choosing to do so.

So even when your lover leaves you, there's no pain?

No. There's no pain when my lover leaves me because I've discovered the beauty and the wonder of who I am. I thought in the old days when my lover left me that my validation and that my idea about who I am was walking out the door with her. I've now learned, and this is going to sound, I suppose in some ways, a bit crass, but it's the truth: when she walks out the door, there'll be fifty more behind her ready to walk in. That's because I'm magnificent.

What role does Nancy play in your career?

I'm going to give you an answer that's like a Divine Dichotomy. She plays every role and she plays no role at all. In other words, I'm very clear that Nancy is not the force in my life that makes my career possible. If I thought that that were true, I'd be back into fear, that if I lost her, all would be lost. So I don't see Nancy as being that element which makes my life, as it's now being lived, possible. And yet, in some very mysterious and interesting way, without her, it wouldn't be possible. So it's a Divine Dichotomy.

The role that she plays in my life, I guess, is that Nancy is the chief person in my life who sees me as I see me. She sees me as I imagine myself to be. Love does that. Love says, "I'm willing to see you as *you* see you in your best version of yourself. And that's how I'm willing to see you." In fact, love says more; love says, "Not only am I willing to see you as you see you in your best version of yourself, I'm willing to see you even as you don't see yourself. I'm willing to see you as *more* than you see yourself."

Someone once said, "If we saw ourselves as God sees us, we'd smile a lot." I think that Nancy sees me as God sees me. She says things to me all the time, little things. She just walked past me a moment ago, and said, "God, you're handsome." You know, I shouldn't tell those tales out of school, I guess, but if I have a thought even for a moment that maybe it's not true, maybe I want to fall back to my prior thoughts about myself, that I'm not physically attractive, people like Nancy, those who really love you, keep you affirmed in your most daring thoughts about yourself.

That's it! That just came through. People who *really* love you keep you affirmed in your most *daring* thoughts about yourself. You *are* it. You *can* do it. You know . . . those daring thoughts that we have in the middle of the night that we don't dare share with anyone else, because they're going to call us this, that, or the other—egotistical, or irresponsible, or whatever they're going to call us—if we let them hear those daring middle-of-the-night thoughts that we have about ourselves. Dare I think this about me? You know, when you're around someone who loves you deeply, you don't have to think these thoughts; they say them for you: "God, you're sexy; God, you're powerful; God, you're good; God, you're wonderful; God, I'm glad you're mine." Nancy says those things to me all the time, every day. Scarcely an hour goes by I don't hear a message of affirmation from Nancy. What role does that play in my life? I don't have words for that.

> *In the book, they talk about finding out what you want—what you want to be, what you want to have, and what you want to do. And in terms of relationships,*

I've taken that literally—by literally writing down the kind of partner that I would like to have. And I found that partners are showing up in ways that weren't the package I thought would show up. And it's kind of confusing, because I'm not sure, you know, whether I should just not sit down and write that out, and look at that as sort of like whatever the universe gives me. And I'd like to ask you to comment on that.

Sure. Thank you. It's a very good question.

With regard to relationships or anything else in life, I like to get very specific about what it is that I would choose. And after I've allowed myself to be very, very specific, *I take what shows up.* And the reason that I do that is that I never stop God from performing the miracles that She devises. And I never try to tell God what something should specifically look like, but merely what my idea about it is, in the moment.

You know, when I was a young man I had an idea of what the perfect mate looked like.

And anyone who did not fit that mold was almost automatically rejected. I mean, I'd literally walk right past them, actually, and pay them no mind, almost as if they weren't there. Then one of those delightful, delicious accidents in life happened. I fell in love with a woman who was quite different from those pictures that I had created. I almost backed in to this particular relationship because, as I said, I ordinarily walked past that kind of a person. But somehow or another, there I was. And in that moment, I saw how extraordinary a human being this was, and how much I had missed in life by insisting that, not just people, but events, you know, places, I mean *everything* in my life, had to be a certain way, you see.

I'd go to a party. If it didn't feel a certain way, I'd leave because it wasn't what I'd expected. I was living my whole life out of my expectations, and most importantly, my relationships with people. And I was really missing such a huge part of it.

Nancy did not fit any of my prior pictures of the kind of woman I thought I would wind up being involved with over the long run, for a whole variety of reasons. She was far more sensible and not nearly as spontaneous as I am, to give you just an example of what I'm talking about, and many, many other things as well. I now see that these differences between us need not create gulfs, nor are they necessarily items that render her "ineligible." You see, in fact, they are aspects of her being that provide a perfect balance to who I am. I would never have seen that in my more immature days, however.

So my best advice to anyone who is seeking a mate, or really looking for anything in life, actually, is to have some idea of what you're looking for, for sure. But notice that sometimes goodness will come to you in packages that are quite unexpected. Do not disallow, or render ineligible, those incoming energies. Because you're liable to find that what you're looking for is right under your nose, and you haven't seen it because your eyes weren't open.

Some of the most wonderful parts of my life have come to me in packages that are most unexpected and would have been called unacceptable just a few years ago. I mean—let me give you a silly example—I eat foods now that I would have called unacceptable even a few years ago. You know what I'm saying? I eat stuff now, and I'm open to it. My mother used to say, "Try it, try it." I never understood the wisdom of that. It's not only wise with regard to food, but with regard to everything in life. For heaven's sake, try it. I mean literally, for *heaven's* sake. Because you might find your own heaven right there. And so, don't get too tied in. And don't get too caught up in your expectations, but leave yourself wide open. And give God some room to create perfection for you.

Now, using again the example of my darling wife, Nancy, and I'm not going to say anything here out of school that Nancy hasn't heard from me privately and directly in our very close moments . . . but when Nancy first showed up in my life, as I said, she did not fit any of the pictures of the person that I would like to spend the rest of my life with. And I dare say that the same may have been true about me for her. I don't know. I never asked her. I know that in my case, she did not show up in the package that I had in my head about what the other person is supposed to look like. But, boy, oh boy, oh boy. The greatest thing I ever did in my life was to say: "You know what, I'm going to just discard my first idea for the moment, and see what kind of gift God has laid at my door." And my willingness to do that has caused me to see that God sent me the greatest treasure my life has ever known.

And now it looks so much like that most treasured thing that, ironically enough, every other person in my life is somehow subtly measured against that. Isn't that interesting? That's probably not very wise of me to do that, but I'm being very transparent with you, just to show you the juxtaposition. It's so funny, but that which was not my picture at one point, has become so much my picture that I now measure everyone else against that—which is equally unfair, of course. And I've got to grow up and stop doing that.

> *What I've noticed in my life—I want to add to what this gentleman just said—is when I used to think I knew who I was looking for and all the qualities, I found that it was these qualities that I thought would make me, or make the relationship, feel a certain way. And then I discovered that, when somebody showed up and the feeling matched what I was trying to get from the package, that was the real value. And it didn't really matter the descriptions of the qualities, just that the feelings matched.*

Yes, that's a very, very insightful and intuitive observation. And I want to share with the room that, while, in my life, I have tried to be as specific as I can with regard to what I want to show up—whether it's a job, or a person, or a new car—in my later years, as I've gotten a bit older, I learned to just drop all of those specific requirements. I've learned to really let go and let God. And I've learned to just notice that miracles come almost inevitably in packages that look quite unlike what I thought the package should look like. And so, I've kind of let go . . . . That's called living your life without expectation.

I think it's important to understand that love is a decision, it's not a reaction. Most people think that love is a reaction. I mean, that's really the main difference between the time when I lived out of expectations and had a certain package in mind, and when I dropped my expectations and found myself relating to people in a whole different way. The difference is that I've learned that love is a decision. You decide to love someone, or you decide not to, and it's really very, very arbitrary. Now one could say, "Yes, of course, but those decisions are based on appearance or personality, and so forth."

But I suggest that they sometimes are not. I suggest that they're sometimes based on something more arbitrary than that: a simple choice. I choose to love you. And when I really love you and come from a love that's pure, not only is my choice arbitrary, but it's unconditional. My love is unconditional. It's not conditioned on how your personality is showing up in this hour, or the shape and form of your body, or the size of your billfold, or anything else that's attendant to you. But, in fact, it does not know condition.

So when we choose to love someone, we are often in for a big surprise. We discover that the feeling we had hoped to get from being in love with the other person is really generated *over here*, and simply comes *to* us, *from* us, around that other person, almost like a planet flies around a sun, and then comes back to the other side in the heavens. It's that boomerang effect. And the great illusion is broken, at last. The illusion being, of course, that the feeling, that feeling of magic and wonderment, and that specialness, that I'm looking for in relationship, is coming from the other person. In truth, it was always coming from here. And when I send it there, and do so quite deliberately, it has no choice but to come back over here. It's like that song, "Return to Sender."

In the days when I wanted things or people or stuff to show up in a particular form, I had to ask myself the question that you're driving at, of course. Why do I have an idea that *that* form is somehow better than another form? Why do I have an idea that thin is better than fat, or fat is better than thin, or black is better than white, or . . . What's my thought about that? What's that about?

As soon as I was willing to address that question, I could see that I was *making it all up*. I was just making all that stuff up. And suddenly I found it possible, when I let go of the things I was making up, to find treasures everywhere; in people that I never thought I could relate to, in things that I never thought I could find a love for. It's like a grown-up discovering that spinach isn't so bad after all.

You know, I've actually discovered that broccoli is an acquired taste. It's now really quite good. So you never know when broccoli will walk through the door.

Are there any other questions in the room about relationship? You all have it pretty well solved, do you? So, how many of you are ready to live in your relationship in a way that says, "My will for you is your will for you?" How many of you are ready to live in a relationship in a way that says to your loved one, "Love never says no?" [Hands go up]

That's great. Almost everyone in the room. Some hands go up just a little more slowly than others. But that's terrific. But please understand that this will not guarantee that the relationship will stay the way it now is. So, don't leave the room, thinking: "I've now just gotten the key. I'm going to live this way. And now my relationship will stay the way it is for evermore." The other person might, in fact, say: "Oh, thank you. Your will for me is my will for me? I'm out of here. My will for me has been to leave here for four years. I've just been waiting for permission." Kind of like, you know, "getting out with honor."

So, I don't want anyone to think that what I'm suggesting is that by living this way, you'll somehow find the guarantee; we've all been trying to find that guarantee. "How can I make it work now and for evermore?" Well, you can't make it work now and for evermore. Or, more correctly, it *will* work, even for evermore, but the way it's working *may be different from the way you think it's supposed to work.*

One relationship that I was in ended, and I called it a tragedy when it ended—my God, I couldn't believe it—because it "looked like" it "wasn't working." And the truth is that it was the ending of that relationship that opened the door to something much more enriching, and much more rewarding, in my life than ever I imagined I could experience. But it was only by allowing that which was going on to go on, and not judge it and make it wrong, and call it a tragedy, but just to simply let it happen, that I was able to experience what was coming to me next. So, I have discovered in my life that the universe works in extraordinary ways, and that if I just don't judge it, and allow it to do what it's doing, and to be what it's being, then I will find the peace and the joy that always resides within me.

And, by the way, I want to say again, that's the largest key, if there is a key: I must stop looking to another for the peace and joy for which I have so long searched, and realize that that for which I have searched resides within me. My grandest joy and my greatest peace is experienced when I provide for another; in those moments, I am unlocking the greatest mystery and the greatest secret of all time.

And again I say, as I said before, here is the grandest irony: That in the moment that I see myself as the Source of that which I would receive from another, and in the moment when I choose to use my life to source that to another, in that moment I come as close to guaranteeing that the room will not empty out as I could possibly ever get. Because nobody leaves the room in which there resides the Source, or very few. And those who do? Let 'em go. Let them walk their path. Let them do what they're doing.

I'd like to go back to the matter of marriage. I've been thinking a lot lately, Neale, about the whole institution of the couple. And I'm very interested by what Book 3 *said. Does marriage, as we have created it, call forth that kind of loving that we want? It seems to me that as we enter the twenty-first century, we're in a different place than human beings have ever been with regard to love and romance. Which is that we don't have to have it be about survival and procreation, which is what we've been up to since the beginning. So, I'm interested in knowing about forms other than the traditional form of the couple in marriage, such as living together, either with or without children, shared survival, that whole form. Are there other forms that we could begin to create that call forth that freedom and commitment, and the best in our loving?*

That's a wonderful question. And the answer is: Yes, there are many other forms now that stand aside from the traditional two-person relationship. We're seeing now intentional communities, in which a large number of people live together in a caring, sharing, and loving way. We're seeing what is loosely called—I know this is a bad word in some places—group marriages, or expanded or extended families, in which people are living together in caring, sharing, and loving ways.

We're seeing same-gender couplings in which people are living together in caring and sharing ways. By the way, if we don't stop making these paradigms wrong, we will never realize our richest and fullest potential as human beings. What happened to Matthew Shepard on that fence in Wyoming cannot and should never happen amongst beings who call themselves socialized and civilized, no matter what their beliefs. It's incomprehensible to me that that kind of behavior could occur, much less be condoned, by even a small portion of society.

I think that couples will always be here. And if you were to ask me if couples will continue to be the primary form of relationship, I believe they will. Always. There's something unique to that circumstance that really can't be re-created in any other form. So I think that always and forever, we'll see two people joining together and co-creating a life, and that will continue to be the primary form of loving human relationship. But, I think we will also see some other forms being created, and those forms will include extended families. They'll include group marriages. They'll include intentional communities. They'll include a variety of ways that people will gather together in numbers large and small to experience the one experience for which we all yearn: the experience of unlimited, unbridled love, one for the other.

We have been experimenting with those kinds of forms for a long time on this planet.

And I think we'll see some of those experiments gain more respectability as people let go of their need to make them wrong. And I think that will happen here as we move into the next century.

The decision to stop making each other wrong for what we're doing is going to be a huge turning point in our social evolution. And that's going to happen here in the next ten to fifteen years—I'm very clear about that. We're going to stop making each other wrong for our sexual lifestyle choices. We're going to stop making each other wrong for our spiritual and philosophical choices. We're going to stop making each other wrong for our political and social choices. We're going to stop making each other wrong for our economic choices. We're going to stop making each other wrong, and simply say, at last, "Can't we just agree that we disagree?"

We're going to stop making each other wrong out of our awareness that making each other wrong is what's killing us, not the points of view that differ, but the fact that we are intolerant of them. Intolerance has seen its final day on this planet. And we're going to see an evaporation of that intolerance, I think, in the first quarter of the next century, to a large degree.

That will happen as a result of the evolution of the species that's being produced by these experimental ways that we are being together, and these new relationships that we are forming. And these relationships will permeate all of society. There will be new relationships in politics, in economics, in religion; new relationships at every level, and, of course, new romantic relationships, as well. So, it'll be nothing to see a man and two women walking down the street, or a woman and two men walking down the street, in what's called a triad relationship, and they're holding hands and walking side by side, and enjoying the hell out of each other. I mean, enjoying the *hell* right *out* of each other.

God says there is no form in which the expression of love which is pure and true is inappropriate. And the way we know that the expression of love is pure and true is that it never seeks nor allows itself to produce damage to another. I put that in the room because there's always somebody from the media, you know, from the far right who says to me: "He's just, he's just . . . giving a lot of people a license to do *anything* . . . he's condoning pedophiles." There's always someone who wants to go to an extreme to make me wrong. And what I'm saying is that there is no form in which a love that is true and pure is inappropriate. And love that is true and pure would not allow itself to damage another, or to take advantage of another, or be abusive to another in any way.

And so, yes, the ways in which we will join with each other in the expression of our grandest idea of love are changing. People who think that the old way was the only appropriate way are having a difficult time with this. And some of them are gritting their teeth, and some of them are making wrong all of these other forms.

You know, there was a time when we were told, and we were seriously told—it wasn't somebody's whacko, way-out idea, but it was seriously held by the largest number of people in our society—that to couple with a person of another *race* was inappropriate. There were times when we were told that to marry and love another of a different *religion* was inappropriate. There are still people in certain races and religions who disown their loved one because their loved one loves another who is not "one of their own." How could we be not one of our own? There's *only one of us*. It's called the Human Family.

Our job as creators of the new society is to put in place a paradigm, a system, if you please, a new social, and spiritual, and political (because much of this is about politics) construction that allows us to simply love each other in a way that feels pure inside of our soul, regardless of gender, or color, or religion, or any other artificially restrictive factor. How can it be wrong to love each other? How can there be a wrong way to express pure love which would never damage or hurt another? Yet, our uptightness about that, based on what we, in our arrogance, presume to be the Will of God . . . I mean, can you imagine a time, and we're not talking about centuries ago here, but a couple of generations back, when we actually stood up and seriously suggested that it was God's law that we should not marry interracially? That it violated the law of God? Help me out. And we actually believed that.

In fact, there are people who still believe it today. I know a Jewish couple who disowned their son for marrying a non-Jew. What's the word they use for it? Gentile, goyim. And they've disowned him because he married outside the faith. What is that? That is a thought that says not only am I separate from you—which is a false-enough thought—not only am I separate from you, but guess what? I'm better than you. We're better than they are. So how could you possibly marry *that*? Those are the kinds of thoughts that have created the kinds of miseries that have been visited upon this planet for lo these many years.

Yet, it is the new understandings that you bring into the new days and times into which we all are now ushering ourselves, that will create a new experience. The world, with regard to the subject we call love, has been waiting for a long time for a savior to come again. That savior has already arrived. She sits right there, and there. [Pointing to members of the audience] And he's right there, and he's there.

Will you save us from our lowest idea about ourselves? And will you take us to our grandest place? We can only go as high as you're willing to go. We can only become as extraordinary as you're willing to be. We can only love as fully as you're willing to love. You're it. You're the one. There are those who see the world as it is, and ask, "Why?" And those that see the world as it could be, and ask, "Why not?" Thanks for listening.

In Closing...

Thank you for taking this journey with me. I know that some of the ideas in this book are "on the edge." Concepts such as "we are all one," "I choose for you what you choose for you," and "love never says no" are not easy to accept. It will take courage to embrace them—and even more courage to implement them. Yet I believe that it will be essential to do so if we are, in the stirring words of Robert F. Kennedy, to seek a newer world.

There are many resources now available to help us with these challenges. Those who wish to explore new relationship paradigms more deeply may find of particular interest two books that I experienced to be both helpful and exciting. They are: *The Future of Love*, by Daphne Rose Kingma, and *Enchanted Love:*

The Mystical Powers of Intimate Relationships, by Marianne Williamson.

Both speak eloquently of the *possibilities* of relationship, the wonder of open-hearted love, and the glory of embracing spirit-to-spirit, as well as body-to-body. Marianne's latest work is especially breathtaking, its sweep at times approaching poetry.

If you are looking for something a bit more experiential, once each year the nonprofit foundation that Nancy and I formed presents a weekend retreat on relationships, *How to Love People and Get Away with It*. Based on the messages in *Conversations with God*, it is designed especially for those who are looking closely at bringing a relationship to an end, beginning a new one, or how to live happily within one. In other words, all of us.

For more information on this annual program, write:

CWG Relationships Weekend
ReCreation Foundation

PMB #1150
1257 Siskiyou Blvd.
Ashland, OR 97520

Many questions on relationships, and, for
that matter, all of the issues covered in the *Conversations with God* material, are addressed in
the regular newsletter of the foundation. We
named the foundation ReCreation because the
message of *CWG* is that the purpose of life is to
recreate yourself anew in the next grandest version of the greatest vision ever you held about
Who You Are. The newsletter contains questions from readers all over the world on how to
do just that. I answer each letter personally. If
you would like to "stay connected" with the en-
ergy of *CWG*, you may obtain a 12-issue
subscription to the letter by sending $35 ($45
for addresses outside the U.S.) to the foundation.

Finally, Hampton Roads Publishing Company has produced a wonderful collection of
the best of these queries and responses over the

past five years, entitled *Questions and Answers on Conversations with God*. It and the *CWG Guidebook* (also from Hampton Roads) are two of the most helpful books ever produced for those who truly seek to understand the *CWG* material more fully, and to find practical ways to apply it in their every day lives.

By these and other means, I hope that we can all learn more about relationships, and how to improve them. I hope that we'll all remember how to love. We knew how to, once. We knew how to live without expectation, without fear, without neediness, and without having to have power over someone, or to be somehow better than another. If we can get back to that place, we can heal our lives, and heal the world.

Blessèd be.

Hampton Roads Publishing Company
publishes and distributes books on a variety of subjects,
including metaphysics, health, complementary medicine,
visionary fiction, and other related topics.

To order books or to receive a copy of our latest catalog,
call toll-free, 1-800-766-8009,
or send your name and address to:

Hampton Roads Publishing Company, Inc.
134 Burgess Lane
Charlottesville, VA 22902

email: hrpc@hrpub.com
web site: http://www.hrpub.com

Neale Donald Walsch on Relationships, Neale Donald Walsch on Abundance, and *Neale Donald Walsch on Holistic Living* are based on the concepts in *Conversations with God,* and are available on audiocassette from your local bookstore or New World Library at 1-800-972-6657 ext. 52, or from their website at nwlib.com.